Loch Lomond

in old picture postcards

by
John G. Danielewski

European Library - Zaltbommel/Netherlands MCMLXXXVII

Life is what happens to you while you're busy making other plans (John Lennon).

GB   ISBN 90 288 4599 2 / CIP

© 1987 European Library - Zaltbommel/Netherlands

European Library in Zaltbommel/Netherlands publishes among other things the following series:

IN OLD PICTURE POSTCARDS *is a series of books which sets out to show what a particular place looked like and what life was like in Victorian and Edwardian times. A book about virtually every town in the United Kingdom is to be published in this series. By the end of this year about 300 different volumes will have appeared. 1,500 books have already been published devoted to the Netherlands with the title* **In oude ansichten.** *In Germany, Austria and Switzerland 650, 100 and 25 books have been published as* **In alten Ansichten;** *in France by the name* **En cartes postales anciennes** *and in Belgium as* **In oude prentkaarten** *and/or* **En cartes postales anciennes** *150 respectively 400 volumes have been published.*

For further particulars about published or forthcoming books, apply to your bookseller or direct to the publisher.

INTRODUCTION

The 650 ft. deep gorge that now accommodates the 27.5 square miles of Loch Lomond was gouged out during a previous ice age. When the ice retreated, the gorge filled with sea water, i.e. a 'marine incursion' took place. According to the recent findings of Dr. Duncan A. Stewart, this marine incursion occurred between 5300-3500 B.C. apart from a period of 30-40 years commencing 4500 B.C. when the loch became land-locked. (The inference being there were two marine incursions separated by the said 30-40 years.) For the 800 year post-incursion period there was a salt water layer in the loch.

Anciently, the lands that are now Dunbartonshire and a fair proportion of Stirlingshire were part of the vast estates of the Earls of Lennox and occasionally the lands are referred to as *The Lennox*. The domains of the Earls extended almost as far eastwards as Kirkintilloch. Apart from the strongholds of the Earls mentioned in the text, there was a Lennox Castle near Ballagan Spout, east of Strathblane and a castle at Mugdock, near Milngavie, later to be the property of the Marquisses of Montrose. Lennox is said to have been derived from *Levenax* (a latinised form of Leven) meaning the field of the Leven or elm tree. Loch Lomond is named after Ben Lomond, from *luman* – a beacon.

There are large numbers of prehistoric and archaeological sites locally, including the iron-age forts at Carman, Craigie Fort (Balmaha) and Cashell; the cairn at Cameron (Ordnance Survey Ref. NS 371821); the two cairns at Inverbeg (NS 345979 and 345981); the cairn and burial mounds at Stuckindroin (NN 323145) and numerous cup and ring marks. Also, there was an old legend of *Dun Lolachrodh* or Castlepool Castle, the site of which is open to speculation, though there is a Lochan a' Chaisteil (NN 343188) – Castle Lochan, and nearby a mountain called An Caisteal. There are also ruins showing that in times past the area was considerably more populated than today. On the east

shore of the loch there were numerous townships of which perhaps only one building on each site remains; the corn kiln at Blairstainge, (NN 324173) is one of the more remarkable vestiges of a former era. The islands, in particular, were all heavily populated. The population has decreased, firstly due to the *clearances* and secondly, due to the work of the gauger ('gayjer') or exciseman in curbing the extensive smuggling and the illicit manufacture of the *Dew of the Mountain,* i.e. whisky, that was carried on well into Victorian times: a three-masted vessel, the *King's Cutter* was stationed on the loch as a deterrent.

For centuries the loch appeared to be rising. In King Arthur's time there is mention of a lake 'which contains 60 islands' half of which have now sunk in the intervening millenium. Further evidence of the rising water level are indicated by sunken ruins which abound the loch. These include the church of *Killdavie* off Inchcailloch (ostensibly they are the ruins of a convent, or both). The ruins of a large sunken building is said to exist 3 km north of the Leven. A silted-over or sunken island existed at the mouth of the Falloch: it used to be an early McFarlane stronghold. The stepping-stones across the Falloch are now under feet of water. The level of the loch is now stable due to the erection of a barrage across the Leven in connection with the 1971 scheme utilising the loch as a reservoir capable of having 100 million gallons per day drawn off via a pumping station west of Ross Priory to serve the needs of Central Scotland. Most visitors are unaware of the loch's status as a major reservoir, supplying about 10-15 m.g.d. more than neighbouring Loch Katrine. But the loch is under threat with the cloud of the Craigrostan water storage hydro-electric scheme still hanging over it. Should it ever be given the go-ahead, one of the last wildernesses of Europe (and attendant wildlife) will be lost forever.

The area is very rich in flora and fauna with nature reserves established on a handful of islands as well as at the mouth of the

Endrick. About 200 species of birds have been identified as have 30 species of mammals (including wallabies kept by a local land-owner on Inchconachan which escaped when the loch froze over giving rise to disbelieved sightings by passers-by who must have been thought of as potty!); whales may have swam on the loch during the marine incursion as whale bones have been found. 550 species of plants (i.e. over 25% of all known U.K. plant species), including a plant unique to the area, the *Loch Lomond Dock,* flourish here. There are large, rare and ancient trees within sight of the loch: on Inchlonaig was Europe's largest yew tree plantation containing many thousands, said to have been planted by Robert the Bruce as a supply of wood for bows and arrows. It is further maintained that Bruce's troops at Ban-nockburn used weapons made from this plantation. There is also a fish that is unique to Loch Lomond (and Loch Eck) which is called the *Powan,* a sort of freshwater herring, which became trapped during the marine incursion and had to acclimatise to the freshwater as the aforementioned salt layer became more and more diluted over the 800 year period. Though very common, the Powan does not yield to rod and line as it is a plankton feeder.

The Lennox is said to have connections with the King Arthur legend: Dumbarton Castle was referred to as *Castri Arthuri* – Arthur's castle – in medieval times, which may have alluded to King Arthur's Royal personnage holding court there. An intriguing theory has been put forward by Count Nikolai Tolstoy (whose grandfather's cousin was THE Tolstoy) that the majician Merlin once frequented the area. Another legend: after the death of Solomon, 10 of the 13 tribes of Israel were exiled by the Assyrians, a 'lost tribe' of which may have settled in the Loch Lomond area. There is evidence that the ancient Egyptians may have known about and visited the loch. The ancient Romans, too, were familiar with the loch, calling it *Lyncaledur* – the lake

of the woody water – a name which invites comparison with the etymological derivation of the terms *Lennox* and *Leven.*

Most people are familiar with the song about the 'Bonnie Bonnie Banks o' Loch Lomond' but may not be too familiar with the legend behind it. It concerns a girl who walked from the loch to Carlisle to see her imprisoned lover who had been sentenced to death for being 'out' during the Jacobite rebellion of 1745. Her lover was reputed to have said *O, ye'll tak' the high road and I'll tak' the low road* (i.e. via the grave) *and I'll* (i.e. his spirit will) *be in Scotland afore ye.*

H.V. Morton in his famous book *In Search of Scotland* (1929) summed it all up about Loch Lomond's 'million beauties', he writes: 'Here is one of the world's glories,' extolling it as the 'greatest of all British lakes.' A curious metaphor was reverted to in Ross's *Loch Lomond and its environs* of 1792, stating that the loch 'presents on the map, something of the appearance of Hercules Club'. Two million people visit this 'Hercules Club' annually, a fair percentage being on day trips from the central belt of Scotland.

This book was originally perceived to include the Trossachs. This has not been practical, however, so the Trossachs is to feature in a separate volume by the author. It is suggested that the reader acquires the *one-inch Trourist Map of Loch Lomond & The Trossachs* or O.S. sheet 56, as a number of O.S. references are given in the text.

The postcards featured are taken from the author's personal collection, and unless otherwise stated, feature turn of the century views. The author is indebted to Graham Hopner of Dumbarton Library; Harry Lynn, Balloch; and especially to Y.F.

Glasgow G33 3QJ   John Danielewski

Balloch.

1. Balloch used to be a small rural community until the opening of the Bowling-Balloch line of the Caledonian & Dumbarton Railway in 1850; the line extended as far as the 1846 Balloch pier. Direct rail link with Glasgow became possible in 1858 when the line joined the Glasgow, Dumbarton & Helensburgh Railway. In the 1870's Balloch was also connected by rail to Stirling; it closed to passenger traffic in the late 1930's and goods in 1957. To further exploit the tourist potential of the area, Dumbarton Burgh and County Tramways Co. Ltd. opened the 11 mile Balloch to Dalmuir West Tramline in February 1907. It was possible to go to Wishaw, 40 tram-miles away from Balloch, though not on the same tram. The Balloch tram terminus was just west of the level crossing. The green and cream liveried trams lost competition to the buses in March 1928. Note the footbridge with its gas lamps, behind which can be seen the gable-ends of the railwaymen's cottages which for fifty years or so marked the westernmost extremity of the village, prior to the building of the three Edwardian houses across the road. Note also that behind the tram of this 1909 view there was open countryside.

41 Balloch Hotel and Bridge

2. The inn featured in this view dates back to 1820, and was built on the site of the Moss o' Balloch farm. The initial function of the inn was to run the ferry, which was pulled across the Leven by chains at the foot of Ferry Loan. A toll suspension bridge was erected by Sir James Colquhoun, 4th Bart., in 1841, being replaced by the current structure in 1887. Among the hotel's guests was Empress Eugénie (wife of Louis-Napoleon, Bonaparte's nephew) in 1860 during her British tour. Said to be in mourning due to the death of her sister, Duchess Alba, the reason for her tour may actually have been appeasement and détant. Ironically, the local Rifle Volunteers, which had been set up to stave off the French threat in those troubled times, was the guard of honour at Balloch. The gable-end on the extreme left was part of a building, demolished in the 1920's, called the Kiln, later Nairn's joinery store, that had the hotel's stables and beer cellar which was connected to the inn by underground lead piping, probably still extant. A dairy and dance-hall were also incorporated; the last dance held was part of the 1918 Victory Celebrations.

Balloch.

3. Both the cameraman and the ice-cream salesman with his wheel barrow appear to be generating some attention from the locals in this turn of the century view. The street scene is recognisable as Balloch's Main Street, also referred to as Balloch Road. The door second from the right was Mrs. McKenzie's, who traded as a newsagents from inside her own home! The building behind the tree, built 1884, is now a bank. Note that Mossview buildings at the corner of Dalvait Road have still to be built. At the far end of the street there appears to be nothing but trees, indicating that Balloch Castle Estate at one time extended beyond the current car-park and bus stance. The trees at the south side of the bus stance bear mute testimony to this effect. Just east of Balloch Estate gates there existed until the end of the 18th century the old schoolhouse of Blackhouseland. Further east at Old Kirk Farm, also known as Shenacles, a large slab that had long been an obstruction to farming was removed in 1969 revealing a bronze age cist containing cremated bone and a food vessel (NS 410839). The site may possibly have been an ancient burial ground.

BALLOCH

4. This view was taken in 1903 immediately after the erection of Mossview Buildings at the corner of Dalvait Road and the Main Street; spoil left over after completion of building work can be seen in the foreground. The Post Office stood at this corner location for around forty years or so. Note the stairs to the front door of what is currently the 'Doghouse', formerly a thatched cottage, and until the 1970's was a café. The Moss o' Balloch is on the other side of the dyke on the right (not to be confused with the controversial *white dyke* separating Balloch Estate from the Moss) where the fair used to be held annually on 15th September. Since 1967 the Highland Games have been staged here. The first of the wooden 'shacks' that became established on the right side of the road was erected in the 1920's. During the war years it accommodated the P.O.; the Tourist House replaced it in the 1970's. The second 'shack' was built in the 1950's to serve as a temporary bank; in 1976 the bank moved across the road. Built into the very fabric of the shack was the former bank's old safe, now put to good use by the current occupiers of the building – a knitwear concern.

MOSS OF BALLOCH FAIR

5. Annually held every 15th September for centuries, the horse fair known as the *Moss o' Balloch* was the most important day of the year in the Vale of Leven (as important as hogmanay), the day being a public holiday. The name of the fair became the name of its venue – the Moss o' Balloch. People and horses would come from all over Scotland to what was 'almost a national institution'. Being both an agricultural and social event, it was 'one of the most popular of its kind held in Scotland'. Quite apart from horse-trading, it featured shooting saloons, merry-go-rounds, helter-skelters (the tower in the background), candymen and women, lucky dips, cheap Jacks or Johns, home-made produce and cookery, apple men (selling toffee-apples, barrow bottom left) 'nymph dancers' and funfair rides. For the day of the fair the excisemen turned a blind eye to unlicensed dealers who erected tents for the sale of whisky and beer. In early Victorian times the caravans were so numerous 'that on being ranged and rigged-out they made a display of scenic grandeur which would have done credit to Glasgow Fair' (then one of Scotland's largest).

6. The Balloch ferry's busiest day of the year was on the day of the fair, with huge queues of people and horses waiting to board. To save space and time it was common practice for the rider to mount his horse and board the ferry. In 1814 a mounted horse was startled and a number of people fell into the river, two of whom died. A dog, whose master had drowned, won the sympathy and endearment of the locals by its incessant pining and yearning and by jumping into the water trying to find him. This statue may commemorate the event. By late Victorian times the fair was in decline: 'neither in numbers nor quality were they equal to collections of previous years' reported the *Lennox Herald* on the 1896 fair. That year the best draught horses were sold for up to £90 and cart horses for £60-£90 (proportionally more expensive than modern family cars, average earnings then were about 10/- or 50p weekly). After a break for the First World War, the last fair was held in 1919, though there was a river carnival in 1920. The Horse Fair served a similar function to a modern-day motor show in promoting personal transport.

7. Balloch is said to mean *the spot where the river leaves the loch*; a previous spelling was *Belach* indicating possible derivation from *bealach* – a pass. Pleasure cruising on the loch has been popular since Victorian times and the Lynn's family concern have been prominent in that field since mid-Victorian times when the firm was founded by Harry Lynn and his son Tom. Initially, the business entailed the haulage of barges up the Leven, later diversifying into the building of steam launches and boats. Harry's grandson, also called Harry, started his boat-hiring business in 1912, eventually acquiring thirty rowing boats and two passenger launches, named Glen Fruin and Glen Douglas. These launches were commandeered during the First World War to ferry troops ashore to the Dardanelles. The boats were replaced by those on the right of this view – Glen Fruin II and Glen Douglas II. The 'shoebox' house boat in the foreground was the *Sonia* belonging to Rudyard Kipling's cousin, Frank. On the extreme left beyond *Monkey Island* was the *Windsor*, one of the houseboats sunk when the *Tea Boat* shown in No. 8 came adrift in a storm. Monkey Island has since been planted with trees to stop it sinking.

BALLOCH SHORE RIGHT-OF-WAY DEMONSTRATION, AUGUST 12th, 1911.

8. For generations the public had enjoyed access to the shore and the right to moor their boats whithout let or hindrance. In the 'Boat Hiring Case', Campbell of Tullichewan, the landowner of the west bank, took out a writ against Sweeney's boatyard preventing boat hire. This was soon followed by an interim interdict ordering Kinloch, the Tea Boat proprietor, to quit on grounds of obstruction, by the trustees of Luss Estates, the landowners of the east bank. Kinloch asserted he was 'merely claiming my right as a member of the public to moor my boat in a position suitable to my requirements,' and considered that his Tea Boat was 'a considerable attraction to Balloch and a factor in its development'. The implications of the landowners' actions caused a furore; a demonstration was planned, which took place on 12th August 1911. According to the *Lennox Herald*, this was attended by 7,000 people. The procession started at Alexandria public park at 3 p.m. On arriving at Balloch the procession split into 3: one division met at the Tea Boat which was used as a platform for speakers, the other two met steam launches opposite Balloch Hotel and Sweeney's boatyard.

Inchmurren Castle

Inchmurrin Island, Lochlomond.

9. When the lands of the Northumbrian Baron, Arkil, were laid waste by William the Conqueror, Malcolm II, as compensation , made him Thane of the Lennox. Alwyn, his grandson, became the 1st Earl of Lennox. The Buchanans, Colquhouns, Galbraiths, McAuleys and McFarlanes were all granted their respective patrimonies from Malduin, the 3rd Earl. Malcolm, 5th Earl, was one of Robert the Bruce's closest friends; he gifted land to Bruce to build Cardross Castle (NS 385758), where Bruce died in 1329. Malcolm was also a signatory of the Arbroath Declaration of 1320. Countess Isabella, daughter of Duncan the 6th Earl, married Regent Albany's son, Murdoch, uniting the Lennox Earldom with the Earldoms of Menteith (Doune Castle) and Fife (Falkland Palace), which were titles also held by Albany, forming the most powerful and extensive of territorial alliances, overshadowing all other Scottish nobility as well as the King. In 1424, James I was released from 18 years of English imprisonment. Feeling betrayed by the Scottish nobles, James had this family executed: Countess Isabella's father, Duncan, her husband Duke of Albany, and her two sons were all hanged at Stirling in 1425.

Old College Arch   Dumbarton

10. Countess Isabella built the Collegiate Church, Dumbarton, by 1450 as a memorial to her dead. It became disused after the reformation and fell into disrepair. The *College Bow*, the last remnant of a once massive pile, was removed in 1850 when the railway came, to the site shown in this view in Kirk Vennel (modern Church Street) becoming the entrance to the old academy. St. Mary's Way now occupy the site. The College Bow was removed to its current site outside the Municipal Buildings in 1907, only yards away from its original location. The Lennox Earldom now became partitioned amongst the descendants of Duncan's other two daughters, Margaret and Elizabeth. Margaret's daughters married *Napier of Merchiston* and *Haldane of Gleneagles* respectively, and were each awarded one fourth of the earldom; Elizabeth's grandson, *Sir John Stewart of Darnley* was awarded the half earldom, including the title of 9th Earl. The descendants of Duncan's illegitimate child, the family of *Lennox of Woodhead*, believe that the earldom should be theirs. A son of the 12th Earl, Henry Lord Darnley, married *Mary Queen of Scots* in 1565, and *from this union the Royal Family have descended*.

Balloch Castle.

2.

11. Prior to 1238 the principal messuage of the Earls of Lennox was Dumbarton Castle which was subsequently resigned to the Crown; Malduin, 3rd Earl of Lennox receiving in exchange Callander Estate nr. Falkirk (later to become the property of the Livingstons in the 14th century). It was around this time that old Balloch Castle, with its stone jetty, was built where the River Leven leaves the loch, commanding access to both the Leven and the country up the loch. Opposite the castle in the middle of the Leven was the now submerged *Cairn Island* – thusly called because a cairn had been erected on it to commemorate the trajic drownings of eleven ladies of the Lennox family whilst bathing from it. During the 1984 drought many boats bottomed on the 'cairn' which had to be bulldozed flat. The castle was abandoned by 1390 to a much safer site on Inchmurren, built from stones of the old castle. After the 15th century partition of the earldom, Balloch was claimed by the Darnleys, who frequently entertained Royalty (and laid out a tennis court). Inchmurren became a hunting lodge frequently patronised by Royalty. Balloch was acquired by the Colquhouns in 1652.

BOTURICH CASTLE

BOTURICH CASTLE, LOCH LOMOND.

12. John Buchanan, on inheriting his father's properties in Ardoch, nr. Gartocharn, and Dalmarnock, Glasgow, in 1789, sought to expand his properties along Loch Lomondside by acquiring Little Boturich and Knockour from the Rouets, Balloch Estate from the Colquhouns (1802) and Boturich Castle from Haldane of Gleneagles (1811). To a design by *Lugar*, Buchanan built the 'Gothic Picturesque' Castle shown in No.11 using stones from the old castle. He also inherited his father's business – Glasgow's largest hat factory, and was a prominent member of Glasgow's first bank, the *Ship Bank* (founded in 1749 in Briggait), run by the dominating Robert *Carrick* of *Carrick-Brown*. Bank notes would be brought to Buchanan by Alex McQuattie for signature then returned to the bank to be countersigned by the accountant. In 1830 Gibson Stott bought the estate from Buchanan, who temporarily stayed at Levenside House, Campbell of Stonefield's property, and built Boturich Mansion (above) in 1834, using the old wall of Boturich castle, where he died four years later. His son-in-law, Robert Findlay, inherited the property and his descendants still occupy it.

Loch Lomond Park —
Loch Lomond with Ben Lomond in distance.

13. Being an affable character, John Buchanan of Balloch allowed the public access to his policies, and would readily enter into conversation with them, some of whom would be invited to his castle for a 'wee dram'. A frequent visitor was Sir Walter Scott during the height of his fame. Wanton vandalism forced Buchanan to erect the *White Dyke*, a whitewashed wall, still extant, separating his land from the Moss o' Balloch. Gibson Stott, the subsequent owner, was said to have 'greatly improved the grounds'. It is likely that most of the mature trees that now adorn the park were planted during his time. Most visitors would be surprised to learn that the lochside path shown in this view is a medieval roadway used by the Lennox nobility and by travellers on their way to and from the Pass of Balmaha. The roadway is still traceable along the south shore of the loch to Balmaha. The estate is currently under a 99 year lease to Dumbarton District Council who use the castle as a visitor centre and as a base for the Countryside Ranger Service.

Cameron House, Lochlomondside.

14. Cameron Estate was once the property of the Dennistouns of Colgrain, after whom a district in Glasgow was named. They sold the estates in 1612, and after a handful of owners it was ultimately acquired in 1763 by James Smollet, Laird of Bonhill, who was a cousin of *Tobias Smollet*, the writer and dramatist. The estate contained an old 14th century keep which had many tunnels and underground passages. In October 1773, Johnson & Boswell paid a visit to the estate and the laird took advantage of this opportunity to ask for Dr. Johnson's advice for a proposed inscription on a memorial column to be erected at Renton to his illustrious kinsman Dr. Tobias Smollet. It was suggested that the inscription be in latin. About 1790, the mansion was enlarged, altered in 1806, and was substantially rebuilt after a fire in 1865. In more recent times, Major Telford Smollet re-introduced bears to Scotland in his Loch Lomond Bear Park. Within the mansion there is a room in which objects are 'seen' which do not exist, but appear real enough to those who may have witnessed these phantom objects. The room is never pointed out to tourists lest their imaginations get the better of them.

AUCHENDENNAN.

15. *Auchendennan-Dennistoun,/ Auchendennan-Righ,/ Auchendennan-Lindsay,/ The best o'a' the three*, was an old rhyme concerning the Auchendennan estates; originally the three estates were a single entity collectively known as Auchendennan Righ, or the *Royal Hunting Field* of King Robert the Bruce during his residency Cardross Castle. Auchendennan Righ was gifted to Dumbarton by a religious establishment at an early date, and by the 16th century was feued out to Andrew Dennistoun. From 1609 it was in the possession of various branches of the Napier family until 1718 when it was acquired by a branch of the Bontines of Ardoch. The Rouet family were subsequent proprietors, and built the Italian-styled mansion of Bel-Retiro, later demolished by George Martin on his acquisition of the Auchendennan-Lindsay portion of the estate, building the mansion shown above a few hundred yards north-west, in 1864, to a design by Burnet. In early life Martin had founded business ventures in India, Philipines, as well as his native Glasgow. After the building's use as a rehabilitation centre in the Second World War, the Trade Unions of the USA gave a substantial grant to modify it as the then World's largest Youth Hostel & Conference Centre.

AUCHENHEGLISH, DUMBARTONSHIRE.

16. Auchendennan-Righ was also known as *Auchenheglish* – the field of the kirk. In 1858, when the mansion designed by Burnet, shown above, was being built by the Brock family (a member of whom was the first manager of the Clydesdale Bank in 1838), an ancient burial ground was discovered containing several stone coffins and a handful of skeletons; a turf dyke enclosing the kirkyard was also located. This long-forgotten burial ground was probably utilised by Clan Colquhoun and was probably last used some time in the 17th or 18th centuries. A few hundred yards offshore are the sunken remains of the kirk that is implicit in the name of 'Auchenheglish'; an iron cross was erected over the ruins last century. Auchenheglish mansion is now the Lomond Castle Hotel. Duck Bay immediately south used to be known as the 'open shore' whereby livestock had access to the drinking water of the loch. The remains of a crannog, which was a common type of dwelling of the celtic peoples, exists submerged within the bay. There are many such crannogs on Loch Lomond.

ARDEN HOUSE, LOCH LOMOND

17. The Act of Union of 1707 allowed Scotland access to English trade routes, an advantage that the Scots were not slow to utilise, in the proliferation of the tobacco trade, for example, which was a major factor in the growth of Glasgow's prosperity in the 18th century; eventually over half of the U.K. total trade in tobacco was controlled by the Glasgow *Tobacco-Lords*, one of whom was George Buchanan, who acquired *Auchindennan-Dennistoun* in 1770, changing its name to *Arden*. Buchanan's father had an estate in Virginia which abutted the estate of the Washington family, whose younger son, George, became president, and whose older son, Laurence, served under Admiral Vernon on the voyage against Carthagena featured by Tobias Smollet in *Roderick Random*. The Washingtons and the Buchanans named their estates after this admiral – hence Mount Vernon in south-east Glasgow acquired by George Buchanan (Sr.) in 1756. Sir James Lumsden bought the estate in 1866, built the above mansion designed by Burnet. As Lord Provost of Glasgow he was knighted by the then Prince of Wales when the memorial stone of Glasgow University was laid in 1868.

BLACK BRIDGE. GLENFRUIN. HELENSBURGH 6.

18. Numerous ruins and traces of a hamlet at Auchenvennal and of a mansion at Ballevoulin (which at one time belonged to an unknown laird) is an indication of the once large crofting community of Glen Fruin. Crofting became uneconomic in the 18th and 19th centuries forcing the locals into the more lucrative smuggling trade and also illicit whisky making in 'sma' stills'. The licensed house at Crosskeys used to sell some of this 'stark naked' i.e. direct from the still. The ever-vigilant excisemen put a halt to these illegal activities thereby destroying the livlihood of the glen's inhabitants and thus causing depopulation. Further evidence of the glen's former large population is shown by the fact that there existed at least two churches, both with graveyards, in the glen. The first was known as *Chapel Diarmid* near Ballevoulin, and the schoolhouse at Kilbride shown above (built 1840) is at, or near, the site of the other, dedicated to *St. Bride or St. Bridget*. Some of the masonry of the actual church is said to have been built into the schoolhouse and also nearby Balimenoch; grave slabs stand beside the schoolhouse.

Glen Fruin,   *Blairnairn* 1890's   Helensburgh.   E 18132

19. Clan Colquhoun and Clan McGregor had been feuding for generations. Many McGregor attrocities including the cattle raid in 1527 by McGregor of Laggerie on Stronerattan (i.e. Strone) farm, Glen Fruin, a Colquhoun property since 1517, forced Mary Queen of Scots (who became a local landowner) to issue *Letters of Fire and Sword* against Clan Gregor in 1563. In 1589 the McGregors murdered Drummond-Ernoch under grizzly circumstances. In 1592 the Colquhoun Clan chief, Sir Humphry, was murdered at beseiged Bannachra Castle, Glen Fruin, by the Laird of McFarlane in which McGregors were in attendance (it had been rumoured to be a reprisal killing for an alleged illicit love affair between Sir Humphry and the Laird of McFarlane's wife). McGregor raids on Glenmullchen and Glenfinlas (1602) in which many Colquhouns were wounded and two killed, brought the matter to a head. The *bluidy sarks* or shirts of the alleged dead and injured were displayed by the 'widows' to a queasy James VI at Stirling who gave the Colquhouns the task of controlling the McGregors.

The High Road, Glen Fruin, *Stroneraltan on far right D (1890's)* Helensburgh. E 1819

20. The McGregors, led by Alasdair the clan chief, arrived at Glen Fruin on 7th February 1603, via Inversnaid, Tarbet, Arrochar and down Loch Longside. The 650 Colquhouns (outnumbering the McGregors 2 : 1) under Sir Alexander, arrived via Glen Luss, Gleann ma Caoruin and Auchengaich Glen straight into an ambush: Ian Dubh nan Lurg (Black John of the mail), Alasdair's brother, with half the McGregors, attacked the rear whilst Alasdair's troops attacked the front. The battle was at its 'hottest' in the vicinity of Strone on the right of this view. Being boggy country the Colquhoun horsemen were almost helpless in the face of the onslaught of McGregor footmen; 140 Colquhouns were killed as opposed to only two McGregors (including Ian Dubh). Sir Alexander was chased all the way back to Rossdhu whilst the McGregors laid waste the Colquhoun lands and stole livestock. James VI by an Act of Privy Council gave the order to 'extirpate Clan Gregour and to ruit oot their posteritie and name'. The McGregors were declared outlaws; their women branded on the cheek or transported to Ireland; their children were left to fend for themselves; the McGregor name was declared illegal. Fifty McGregors, including Alasdair, were later executed at Edinburgh.

Ross Dhu House, Loch Lomond

21. The Colquhouns of Luss owe their first advancement to Malduin, 3rd Earl of Lennox, who granted Umfridus a charter to the lands of Old Kilpatrick. The original castle of Colquhoun was at Middleton, north of Milton, then they moved to Dunglass, the site now being surrounded by the oil terminal at Bowling; Auchentorlie House now stands on the old Colquhoun estate of Silverbanks, of which little trace remains. The 4th Laird, Sir Humphrey, for his loyalty to Bruce, obtained a charter for the lands of Luss, and his successor consolidated his inheritance by marrying 'the fair maid of Luss', heiress of the ancient family of Luss, and settled down to a 12th century castle on Eilan Rossdhu, which was later replaced in the 15th century by a castle on the mainland. One of the visitors to this castle was Mary Queen of Scots on 15th July 1563. In the next century, this castle was invaded by Cromwell's troops. The mansion, shown here in 1894, was built about 1773 and the old castle was deserted. The laird's wife, Lady Helen (after whom Helensburgh was named), shed a tear when she moved from her 'lucky hole' to the modern mansion, where her ghost is said to haunt.

Gallowhill

22. Clan chiefs and feudal overlords had the power of life or death against wrongdoers; this was an intrinsic part of the feudal system that was to last well into the 18th century. Local geographical features were used for the open-air courts – *Tom-na-mhoid* and the gallowshill – *Tom-na-croich*. This view shows the gallowshill of clan Colquhoun which is situated about 1 km. north of the junction with the B832 Helensburgh Road. The courthill is adjacent. It was from a Caledonian Pine tree at the apex of the hill that summary justice was meted out to the two McGregors who stole the sheep which led to the Glen Fruin Massacre; their heads were later hung on stakes outside Rossdhu Castle. A descendant of the 'gallowstree' is shown here. Immediately north of gallowhill was the muster-place of the clan Colquhoun. The site of the McFarlane's gallowshill was on the hillside above the Free Church Manse at Tarbet. Catter Castle was the principle seat of jurisdiction of the Earls of Lennox. The gallows-stone used to be adjacent to Catter House (near the junction of the roads to Drymen and Gartocharn) on the *moot-hill* or court hill of Catter.

INCH GALBRAITH. LOCH LOMOND.

23. Until relatively recent times, most families were large due to poor life expectancy: a large family would therefore ensure probagation of family name and estates. For example, in the late 12th century, Alwyn, the 2nd Earl Lennox had at least ten offspring, each of which when married would insist on having their own castle or fortress. Gilchrist, a younger son of the Earl, therefore built his *Bhreatnachs* fort on the site of a prehistoric lake dwelling in *Inchgalbraith*. Clan MacFarlane and clan Galbraith were related to Gilchrist and in time Inchgalbraith castle and Bannachra castle on the Fruin water, which belonged to another member of the Lennox family, became the strongholds for generations of Galbraiths. The Galbraiths were a troublesome clan who made enemies of their neighbours, the Colquhouns and the Buchanans. One Galbraith in particular, caused so much ill will by his incessantly plundering the larders of Rossdhu Castle that a net was laid out catching the perpetrator as he attempted to swim home to Inchgalbraith. He met with summary justice at Gallowhill.

"KERR AND HIS FOLLY".
BANDRAY. LUSS. LOCH LOMOND. N.B.

24. A number of legends have grown round this statue, nick-named 'Wee Peter', the most saddening of which was that this monument had been raised to the memory of a drowned child. Another story credits it to a wealthy man adopted in his childhood by an Australian, to mark the spot of their fortuitous chance meeting. In actuality, the statue was erected by a William Kerr, an orphan brought up in Luss, who went to London and made his fortune as a stone mason. The statue was originally intended to be part of a building in Balham, London, but was unwanted by the buyer. The statue lay in Mr. Kerr's yard for quite some time before it was finally brought here to Bandry Bay and erected about 50 yards offshore (1890). The patron saint of Luss, *St. Kessog*, was said to have sufferred martyrdom at Bandry in the 6th century. His body was embalmed in sweet herbs (called *Lus* in the gaelic – thus giving the parish its name). Another legend alludes the naming of the parish to the fleur-de-lys (luce) strewn on the coffin of Baronness McAuslan which took root and helped to quell a plague. A cairn which had been dedicated to the saint's memory was removed in the mid-18th century on the building of the military road, unearthing a large stone effigy, presumably that of St. Kessog (NS 358900).

Remains of Floating Island, Luss Straits

25. The old legends of Loch Lomond are expressed in the following rhyme: *Waves without wind, fish without fin, and a floating island.* The 'waves without wind' may be attributable to local earth movements as the highland boundary fault runs through the loch; the finless fish may be Paones, a type of snake, swimming from island to island; the third part of the rhyme was always thought of as a legend. But, in 1583, the French translator of Boece wrote: 'Amoung the islands of Loch Lomond is one which floats upon the water, so that the shepherds who one day have erected their huts and pens for their sheep on one side of it find themselves on the morrow on the other side, by the impetuosity of the winds, which rushing, it is said out of the caverns of the earth, put the lake into violent commotion.' Waldegrave reports an island that 'moves by the waves of the water, and is transputted sometimes towards one point and otherwhiles towards another.' Yet another attributes the legend to a crannog built by Keith MacInDoill who allegedly also built the Giant's Castle at Strathcashell in the 5th century (NS 394932). The above view was taken prior to 1877 by G. W. Wilson, photographer to Queen Victoria.

CAMSTRADDEN BAY

26. Sunk into this bay are said to be the medieval ruins of the old *tower of Camstradden* with its orchard. The modern mansion of Camstradden was built as a replacement by the 12th Laird of Camstradden in 1739. By 1868 the ruins were said to be a pile of stones and were visible when the water level was low. At one time there was a ford between the mainland and Inchtavannach, but the water level here is now quite deep. Prominent on the hillside in this view is one of the slate quarries dating back to the early 16th century and was at one time very important for the local economy, the workers being housed in the 'town of Camstradden', later known as Halfway, until about 1698. Very little remains of this township. The estate of Camstradden was purchased by the Colquhouns of Luss in 1826, and this consolidated the growth of nearby Luss village, where the workers were later housed. At its height, in late Victorian times, the quarries employed 30 men, quite apart from the boatman and labourers who transported the stuff. 800,000 slates averaging 9ins by 6ins, and costing between 15/- (75p) and £2 per thousand were produced annually, mainly for the Glasgow market.

Established Church, Luss

Valentines Series   21358

27. In a 13th century charter Malduin, 3rd Earl of Lennox, confirmed patronage to the church of Malduin, Dean of Lennox and his son Gillemore, a privilege later transferred to the Colquhouns of Luss. Bishop John Cameron of Glasgow is recorded as having built a *theekit* church (i.e. a plain thatched building) at Luss in 1430. Dedicated to St. Kessog, this church was recognised by the McFarlanes of Arrochar as their Parish Church, much to the dissatisfaction of the lairds of Colquhoun. On a hill outside the village, Cnoc-an-Airm, *the hill of arms*, the McFarlanes left their armaments under guard prior to attending services. By 1734, the McFarlanes had built a church of their own at Arrochar. A replacement for the *theekit* was built in 1771. As the village expanded the church became too small, the minister resorting to standing in the doorway to preach to the congregation inside and the overspill outside. During the era of the *resurrectionists*, a tent was erected in the churchyard with two parishioners each night on guard. As a memorial to the laird, Sir James, this church was built in 1875.

LUSS, LOCH LOMOND

28. There appears to be a legend that in medieval times the old village of Luss sank into the loch as a result of an earthquake, and an old pile of stones just offshore, known as the *Old Church*, is offered as proof of the legend; but these stones may be part of an ancient crannog (another crannog exists in Camstradden Bay, 1 km south). Nevertheless, there has been a village at Luss since at least the 13th century. By the 1850's this ancient village with its 'picturesque, thatch-covered, damp, uncomfortable cottages' were razed to the ground. This view by Bauermeister shows a remnant of the old Luss: in the centre is the old drover's inn (Elmbank), the village's oldest building. 'We were glad,' wrote Dorothy Wordsworth who was a guest here in 1803 with her brother William and Coleridge, 'that we were to have such pleasant quarters. It is a nice looking white house by the roadside.' A 'barefooted lass' served them 'poor dinner and sour ale'. As the chilly evening wore on the landlady denied their request for a fire: 'the most cruel and hateful woman I ever saw,' commented Dorothy.

Luss, from the Pier

LUSS FROM THE PIER LOCH LOMOND. 4587. G.W.W.

29. This view shows how much, or rather how little, the village has changed since about 1877, the date of this view by George Washington Wilson. There has been a pier at Luss since 1850, at the beginning of the decade that was to see the current village rising from the rubble of the old. Provisions would now be brought into the village via the steamers, instead of by 'scows' as was the previous practice using a small jetty, the remains of which can be seen in this view. On the pier used to be a general store that was claimed to sell 'a wee drop of everything'. The old Main Street of the village ran behind Cleveland Bank, the building in the centre of this view, parallel with the shore, and running north-south through the village at right-angles to Pier Road. Almost immediately above the figures opposite the pier shed is a cottage with its gable-end to Pier Road. This cottage, complete with garden, used to front the old main street, and, along with neighbouring Sunnyside Cottage and Rose Cottage etc. to its right were built in the 18th century and are the oldest cottages in Pier Road. At one time every garden fronting the shore had an ancient tree growing in it.

LUSS FROM PIER, LOCH LOMOND.

30. To supplement income, tennants during the summer would sleep in tents whilst letting out the cottage for bed and breakfast. The tent shown here at Cleveland Bank may also have been left over from a fair which was held here during special occasions such as the May Day festival (when children would dance round the Maypole), or the Summer Gala, or the annual fair. The right to hold annual fairs in the village was granted by an Act of Parliament in 1695 whereby the Laird of Colquhoun and Luss could stage a weekly market at Luss and four fairs annually each of three days' duration. Since 1850 the sheep fair was held on the third Tuesday of August. Cleveland Bank was also a Post Office at one time, being moved here from the old toll house, which served as the village Post Office during the Victorian era. Note the boats on the shore in this 1894 view by Valentine. At one time every family in the village had a boat for fishing the loch or for hiring out to tourists. It is interesting to note that Luss village enjoys the privilege of sanctuary ('gyrth') granted by Robert the Bruce to his close friend Malcolm, 5th Earl Lennox, in 1315.

The Village of Luss, Loch Lomond. E 25106

31. The village of Luss is said to be the most beautiful in all Scotland. The architectural style of the village was said to have been influenced by a holiday that a dowager Lady Colquhoun made to France. When the pier was built, the time seemed right to construct Pier Road with these cottages to house the estate workers, the quarry workers, and members of Clan Colquhoun (who were usually given priority). The cottages at the foot of Pier Road (Sunnyside Cottage, Rose Cottage, etc.) underwent detail changes to make them conform to the same overall architectural strategy. A very proud dowager Lady Colquhoun of a later generation would personally ensure that all the gardens were spick and span, neat and tidy and that nothing was even an inch out of place. More recently the village was allocated E.E.C. funding for improvements and modernisation. In pre-industrial revolution times, the mainstay of the economy was weaving, and, by 1790, a cotton-mill had been established employing about 35 people. The local quarries in later years superceded weaving as the major source of employment. To accommodate the expansion of the 1850's, a meal mill and a saw mill were in operation.

Luss from North-West

32. This is another of George Washington Wilson's views from his 1877 listings, showing Luss from *Cnoc-an-airm* on the Glen Luss road. The building in the foreground is the primary school and although the number of pupils have dwindled since Victorian and Edwardian times (when the school population peaked at over 100) the school has undergone expansion. Beyond the roofline of the school, one can see that Murray Pl. and Glenburn Cottages have still to be built, and that the area was grazing land for the residents' livestock. 20th century mod cons such as running water came to the village in the 1930's when the old coalhouses were converted to kitchens. The authoress Margaret Cameron of Sunnyside Cottage points out that previously domestic washing and laundry etc. were carried out in wooden tubs under the yew trees! Hygiene too was a problem: for generations the Luss Water was used for dumping rubbish and household refuse, etc. Note the island of *Fraoch Eilean* just offshore with its mature trees: these were burned down in the inter-war years. The island has relatively recently began to recover from its subsequent bald appearance.

Luss Hotel

33. After the 1850's expansion of the village, the old inn was considered to be inadequate in coping with the then increasing population and with the tourists who were 'discovering' Loch Lomond. At that time the Loch Lomond & Trossachs Tour was gaining popularity: this entailed travelling by steamer on Loch Katrine to Stronachlachar, then by coach to Inversnaid to catch the Loch Lomond steamers and disembarking at will; Luss was a popular stop. As it was impractical to expand the old inn, a new structure was built in the 1860's on the outskirts of the village. A map of the military road drawn up by Taylor & Skinner in 1776 shows this inn with a road leading diagonally down to Luss Kirk. The new building erected was probably the portion with the slightly lowered roofline between the middle and right chimney stacks. It had undergone considerable expansion by the time this view was taken in about 1894. Most of the deliveries to the hotel were made via the steamers: it was a welcoming sight to the locals to see the unloaded barrels of beer being rolled up Pier Road to the hotel, which was the focal point of village social life.

Luss from the Heather Island

34. It was in Glen Luss, behind Luss village in this 1870's view, that one of the most infamous events in Scottish social history had their origins. The coarse-haired black-faced sheep was first introduced into the Highlands here in Glenmallochan farm in 1749 causing eviction of the population in what came to be called the 'clearances'. People were forced into a change of diet: mutton instead of beef (which became a luxury item); Scotch Broth, using mutton, was 'invented' and haggis was imported from England. Other apparently 'Scottish' items were foreign in origin: the bagpipes came from Greece, and the kilt was said to have been invented by an Englisman – one of General Wade's roadbuilders! In 1838 when Glenmallochan farm was undergoing rebuilding, the nearby medieval ruins of St. Michael's Chapel was used as a source of building material until the intervention of the laird, Sir James Colquhoun. The opportunity was then used to excavate the pre-reformation chapel: an arched stone vault with narrow lancet openings was discovered as well as such artifacts as a cross, a font, and gold and silver coins dating to James IV's reign (1488-1513).

Inverbeg Inn.

35. As mentioned in the introduction, King Arthur may have held court in Dumbarton, the most northerly part of his kingdom. He had besieged the islands on Loch Lomond to which had retreated a large number of Picts who had harassed his subjects. An army under the Irish King Guillamurius, which was sent to relieve the besieged Picts, was defeated by King Arthur in Glen Douglas. In the 15th century, there were a number of sheilings scattered around the promontory of *Inverbeg*, called Lower Inveruglas in those days. The *Ferry Inn* of Inverbeg shown here was built about 1814. In 1865 the lessee was a John McFarlane. John Robertson was the tennant landlord from 1889 until 1918, when it was taken over by Miss Jessie Martin. Robert Kerr, Luss policeman, took the option of buying the hotel in 1953 after holding a 15-year lease, his son Alistair succeeding him in 1968. Jack and Jennifer Bisset, the current owners, rebuilt the present structure after a fire in 1978. Next door are the 'Internationally renowned Art Galleries' of Alistair Kerr. One mile north of Inverbeg, 600′ above the road, is the *Fairy Loch*. Note, in the foreground, the use of an upturned boat as a hen-house.

BRUCE'S YEW LOCH LOMOND

36. In 1306 King Robert the Bruce met with two defeats in a row: the first was at Methven Wood by the Earl of Pembroke; the second was at Dalrigh by McDougall of Lorne trying to avenge the death of Red Comyn at Bruce's hand. Safety for his 200 followers now lay across the waters of Loch Lomond, but the problem was transportation. Sir James Douglas, one of Bruce's closest friends, saved the day: he found a leaky boat which could hold three at a stretch. Bruce, Douglas and an oarsman tested the boat's viability by trying to reach the west shore whilst baling out the water. Ferrying back and forth, it took a whole night and a day for the 200 to cross, some finding it quicker to swim. Tradition ascribes this as the yew tree by which Bruce entertained his troops with tales of valour and a singalong whilst waiting until the last of his men were safely across. It is situated at *Stuc an t-Iobairt* (pronounced stookan cheepurt), about 100 yards south of Firkin Toll House (NN 334012). It was quite old even in Bruce's day. The rivers *Douglas* and *Inveruglas* ('mouth of the Douglas') marked the boundary of land notionally gifted to Sir James Douglas by Bruce for procuring that boat.

STUCKGOWN HOUSE, TARBET, LOCH LOMOND.

37. The lands of Stuckgowan (meaning New Oak Cottage) were granted to a son of the MacFarlane Clan Chief, whose descendants held the lands for several generations, until 1739 when they were sold to a Mr. Syme (or Simon). Towards the end of the 18th century, the estate was acquired by the McMurrich clan, whose history goes back to 1182, when Mureach, a descendant of an Irish King, came to the Lennox. The McMurrichs reclaimed about fifty acres of the rocky and woody wilderness of Stuckgowan, and built the Regency Gothic villa shown above, now a listed building. Lord Jeffrey was invited by the clan chief to be his guest, where the literary critic stayed annually between 1822 and 1838. Nowadays the property is owned by Luss Estates, with Captain Colquhoun, the brother of the Laird of Luss, in residence since 1945; the establishment is now run as an hotel. The estate has some remarkable arboreal specimens: a Monterey Pine of 120′ in height; the largest Coast Redwood in Scotland at 150′; and a Giant Sequoia, approaching 170′, challenging the record for the tallest tree in the UK. About 500 yards or so south-west on the hillside are the ruins of the *Black Village* whose inhabitants were wiped out by a plague in the 17th century.

Tarbet Hotel

38. There has been a coaching inn at Tarbet since the 1570's. It has played host to such worthies as Dr. Johnson (1773), Wordsworth & Coleridge (1803), and Rabbie Burns (1787), who dedicated a poem to the inn-keeper's daughter. He had spent most of the night singing and dancing and commented that the local ladies 'sang like angels'; at dawn he went outside where the view shown in no.39 awaited him; he was so impressed to see 'the glorious lump of day peering over the towering top of Benlomond' that he fell to his knees in humble veneration. Later that day on his way back to Dumbarton he was somewhat miffed at being outgalloped by a 'Highlandman', that Burns and his friend, Donald, gave chase, overtook him, and the two hapless companions collided with each other, the horse throwing Donald's 'breekless backside into a clipt hedge'! The current frontage to the hotel was built in 1882 under the managership of A.H. McPherson, and was known as the *Colquhoun Arms*. In 1904, the Tarbet Hotel Co. was formed to look after the interests of the establishment. John and Jean Galbraith, owners since 1967, totally refurbished the hotel internally, adding an extension in 1974.

6448-5   BEN LOMOND FROM TARBET.

39. The lands of Arrochar, which stretched from Tarbet to Ardlui, were granted by Malduin, 3rd Earl of Lennox, to his brother Gilchrist, between 1225-1229. His great-grandson Bartholemew, whose name was Parlan in the Gaelic, gave clan McFarlane its name. The original clan residence was at Clattachmore, now the manse site (NN 320047), and their old tower of Tighrechtichan was west of Tarbet. Their earliest island castle was at Inveruglas, later blown up by Cromwells troops. Recently an old sword and the keys to the main door were recovered from the castle ruins. By 1577 the clan had built a castle on Eilan-a-Vow, opposite which on the mainland, was situated the 16th century almshouse of *Croiteaphurte* (pronounced crutafoorsht: NN 327129) used for embarking and disembarking from their island home, as well as providing accommodation for travellers. In 1697 a modest mansion at Inverioch, Arrochar, became the chief seat of the clan; it was sold to Ferguson of Raith in 1785 along with the attendant lands. The land is now part of Luss Estates. Until the 1930's there was a horse coach service, an example being shown above, between Tarbet pier and Arrochar pier to link with the Glasgow steamers. The meadow in the foreground is currently being landscaped.

The Still Brae and Smithy, Tarbet, Loch Lomond.

40. The *Still Brae* is situated about 100 yards north of the hotel. In this view, the building on the left was erected in 1745 as a distillery, which was an extension of a 1735 building, just out of shot on the left. Local grain was used in the whisky production which was exported out of the locality for consumption. Window tax made glass rather costly, causing closure of the distillery due to lack of bottles. Since those days, the building has housed an undertaker and joiner, a plumber and a weaver. The A82 Loch Lomond Road can be seen at the bottom of the brae. During the reign of King Haco of Norway, a fleet of some sixty ships were sent into Loch Long, laying waste the country alongside (summer 1263). Smaller boats were then dragged across the narrow isthmus between Arrochar and here at Tarbet, into Loch Lomond, by-passing the impregnable fort of Dumbarton, set fire to the islands, which in those days were heavily populated, put to the sword as many of the locals as they saw fit, and left cottages and castles in ruins. Forced to retreat because a storm had destroyed a number of their boats, the Vikings were finally defeated on the Clyde near Largs. The 'pencil' monument on Bowen Craig at Largs commemorates this battle.

ARROCHAR, HEAD OF LOCH LONG   27338

41. Arrochar, which may mean 'a portion of land' or 'hilly country' was named after the parish of the same name, which for about five and a half centuries was the patrimony of clan McFarlane. The Cobbler Hotel is built on the site of the clan chief's castle of *Inverioch*. Arrochar village used to be a mainly crofting community. In this 1897 view, Craigard stores now occupy the site of the thatched cottages in the foreground on the far side of the road. To their right is Tigh-na-Clach (about 1877) which was also the name of a former smiddy that used to exist across the road in what is now the car park of Loch Long Hotel (formerly Ross Hotel). In collaboration with the goblin of the nearby curative well at Glenloin the smithy made a lucrative living curing ailments: the patient, on giving the smithy a silver coin, got in return a special magic nail which had to be hammered by the patient into a tree-trunk adjacent to the well in question and the water of the well drunk. A cure for the patients's ailment was thus guaranteed. One day the goblin found human waste in his well; he became so incensed that he took away the well's curative ability (so says the legend).

42. In this view of Arrochar of 1897, the crofts in the right foreground were the Craigard cottages, diagonally across the road from the *Crazy House*, which was used by the Polish troops, who were stationed at Argyll during the Second World War. It served as a temporary village hall which must have been reroofed with thatch as it caught fire from a spark of a passing steam lorry in 1946. The site is now a car park immediately south of Belmont. Greenbank at the end of the street is still recogniseable; to its right is Johnie Jackson's bakery. A dairy was later built above it. An English tourist staying at an adjacent building in the 19th century asked his landlady for a hot bath. The only vessel available had been a cauldron used for tanning nets. After the bath, the tourist found his skin well and truly tanned, and oh horrors! it would not wash off! On his return home, the tourist's friends were amazed at his rich 'sun tan' – acquired in Scotland of all places! The Moorings now occupy the site of the bakery/dairy. Across the loch, behind the twin-masted sailing ship and south of the site of the old inn of *Alt-na-Gall*, has, since 1910, sprang up the Admiralty torpedo range, now a large establishment.

PULPIT ROCK, ARDLUI, LOCH LOMOND.

RELIABLE SERIES 608 / 23

43. 'Build me a Pulpit and a Vestry and I will come at certain dates and preach to you,' was the reply of Reverend Peter Proudfoot, minister at Arrochar, to those who complained about the distance they had to travel in order to attend a service from the northernmost parts of the parish. So in 1825, financed by Watson of Glenfalloch and Grieve of Keilator, the congregation hewed out of the face of this 28,000 ton rock an opening large enough to hold the minister, an elder and the precentor. A Robert McFarlane, who used explosives in the work, was blinded; from then on he was know as 'Blind Rabbie'. The vestry was reached by a flight of steps and had a wooden door, the iron hinges of which are still visible today. For about 70 years services were held on a monthly basis during the summer. Usually there were about 100 of a congregation who sat on turves on the ground around the rock, where, for most of the following week the proceedings ensued in an almost carnival atmosphere. A stall was set up behind the rock selling bread, cheese and whisky prompting a leading citizen to comment: 'The Lord is at the front, but the Devil is behind.'

ARDLUI HOTEL, LOCH LOMOND

44. This view shows Ardlui Hotel from the south west. The central portion, which used to be a Colquhoun hunting lodge, may date from 1851. By 1886, it was opened as a hotel by D. M. Dodds, and two years later, the east wing was added, while the west wing was added by 1905. Tennants since 1959, Brian and Anne Squires have owned the hotel since 1978, and amongst their 'Guests' is a mischievous ghost described as Spanish-looking, with a tanned complexion, aged about 25, wearing 18th century dress. Only the head, arms and chest of this ghost are visible, and included in the tricks it gets up to, is making thumping sounds as if walking heavily, flushing the WC's and banging toilet seats! In 1847, to facilitate passenger steamer traffic to the 17th century drover's inn of Inverarnan, and thus connect with coaches northwards, a 2-mile length of canal, resplendent with basin and pier, was dug under the supervision of Finlay Ferrier. During the excavation of the canal, several old claymores were found, indicating that a clan battle may have taken place in the vicinity. The Waterwitch was the first paddle-steamer to use the canal, which is now not navigable due to it being used as a rubbish dump.

Rob Roy's Cave, Loch Lomond.

45. Situated one mile north of Inversnaid, this large cavern with a small opening was originally called Bruce's Cave, after the Scottish patriot, who, while being chased by his enemies, sought shelter here. On entering the cave, he heard the sound of breathing and thought he had fallen into a trap; but the breathing belonged to some wild goats and not to his enemies. The goats were a godsend: by snuggling up to them he had a warm en comfortable night. He was so grateful that he granted these goats Royal Protection. Descendants of these humble creatures still roam free today. Well, that was one version of the story. Four centuries after Bruce's day, Rob Roy would use this cavern as a place of concealment with about twenty of his men. From this cave he held his levées, summoned councils of war, and arranged methods of collecting revenue and supplies. Another cave, called smuggler's cave, is nearby (NN 335135). Two miles beyond Rob Roy's Cave, at Pollochro opposite Eilan a Vow, there used to be Sandy Lindsay's Boatyard.

Inversnaid Hotel - shown here in it's role as a Coaching Inn   Loch Lomond

46. Inversnaid Hotel was *not* built on the site of the mansion of Rob Roy (the self-styled 'Baron Inversnaid'), as is the popular legend. Inversnaid proper is about one mile inland where the Snaid Burn meets the Arklet Water (thus the Falls of Inversnaid should theoretically be called the Falls of Inverarklet). The site of Rob's house was about one mile north-east of the hotel, on the west Bank of the Snaid Burn. In August 1803, Wordsworth and his sister, Dorothy, stayed at the ferryman's inn, beside the falls, whilst drying out their clothes during a wet day. It was here that Wordsworth became smitten by the ferryman's daughter who attended them, and wrote a poem about her: *Sweet Highland Girl, a very shower / Of beauty is thy earthly dower!* She was said to be a McFarlane who resided at Corriearklet (where Rob Roy got married in 1693) and she later married a Buchanan. In 1873, then in her 80's, she was still 'singularly handsome' having vibrant eyes and jet-black hair. The building that was eventually to become Inversnaid Hotel was built about 1820, consisting then of the two-storey section on the right of this late Victorian view. During its days as a hunting lodge the former *Garrison* nearby became 'a kind of an inn'.

Arrochar Mountains and Inversnaid Hotel, Loch Lomond *looking to Inveruglas*　　　Valentines Series

47. This 1880 view shows the 'Arrochar mountains' without the unsightly pipes and electricity pylons associated with the Loch Sloy/ Inveruglas power station. Loch Sloy was chosen for expansion to reservoir status because of the high annual rainfall of around 130 inches. The level of the loch was raised 145 ft through damming, resulting in an increase from its original length of a half mile to around two miles, submerging the old clachan of Loch Sloy. Loch Sloy (the clan McFarlane warcry) gave rise to the clan motto of 'This I'll defend' when a pursued clan chief swam to a rock in the middle of the loch and jeered his pursuers with taunts of 'This I'll defend'. Loch Sloy water is now tunnelled through Ben Vorlich (the mountain on the right, inside which, according to legend, exists a huge cavern) then via the aforementioned piping to the power station which was opened by the Queen Mother in 1950. In Victorian times when one wanted to cross to Inversnaid from the west shore one had to blow an old coach-horn, or fire a shotgun or light a smoky fire in order to attract the attention of the ferryman at Inversnaid.

608/134 Rob Roy's Prison, Loch Lomond

48. Not to be confused with the more famous Rob Roy's Cave. Rob Roy's Prison is a rock which rises sheer from the lochside and attains a height of thirty feet or so, having a flat top, which projects from another steep rock of greater height. From the flat top, it was said, Rob Roy would fix a rope round the waist of his adversaries, creditors and debtors and he would then proceed to dunk them in the loch below. Those who would refuse to agree to his demands were then let down again, but this time with the subtle hint that if they remained stubborn and not agreed to his terms when drawn up, the rope would then be tied round their necks, and in this manner would be dunked yet again. Rob Roy invariably got the settlement he asked for, as his antagonists knew they could only escape from this rock or 'prison' by diving into the loch. The ley-line phenomenon by which prehistoric mounds, castles, churches etc., all appear to lie on a straight line, was 'rediscovered' by Alfred Watkins in 1920. The *old straight track to Iona* (Harry Bell, *Forgotten Footsteps*, 1977) is a ley-line running through Stirling Castle - Ben Lomond - Rob Roy's Prison - Arrochar-Inverary-Iona.

R OWARDENAN HOTEL.

49. There has been a hostelry at *Rowardennan* (St. Adamnan's Point) since at least 1696 when a Crown charter was granted to the 3rd Marquis of Montrose. It was a droving inn and howff, i.e. a place of sustenance and refreshment, and was a thatched building in those days. The hostelry remained in the hands of the Ducal family of Montrose until acquisition by Montrose Estates in 1926. Charles M. Collins of the famous Glasgow based publishing empire (which held the world record for publishing bibles) bought the property in 1931. Since then there have been a string of owners: Thomas Kerr in 1950; Henry Linden in 1970; Rowardennan Hotel Ltd. in 1972, and from 1975, Bob and Jean Nicoll, the current owners. Note the wooden building on the left which was originally a church for the convenience of guests (similar wooden structures for religious use were erected at isolated spots in the Highlands: Inversnaid Hotel had a smaller structure). This wooden shack later became the Post Office, and more recently it was moved to the back of the hotel where it became the cook's house (it was burned down in 1983). The oldest part of the hotel is probably the section to the right of the entrance.

Ascending Ben Lomond.

50. The western half of *Ben Lomond* (Scotland's most southerly Monroe) was part of Rob Roy's *Inversnaid & Craigroystan* estates of nearly 7,000 acres acquired in 1693 and containing about 8-900 people living in such long-gone clachans as Doune, Pollochro, Stucnaroy, Cailness, Rowchoish, Knockyle, etc. At the beginning of the 19th century, Sir James Colquhoun invited Sir John Murray McGregor (both were their respective clan leaders) to Rossdhu where they visited the Glen Fruin battlesite and shook hands in reconciliation as the two clans had been feuding for centuries. They climbed up Ben Lomond and the flirtatious Sir John, though in his 80's, still had enough energy to dance a Highland reel with the Colquhoun ladies at the summit (after all, didn't he have Rob Roy's blood coarsing through his veins?). In Victorian and Edwardian times Rowardennan Hotel would hire out ponies to take tourists to the summit of Ben Lomond, the charges (which included a man to lead them, as shown above) were 8/- (40p) to residents, and 10/- (50p) to non-residents.

Pass of Balmaha

Valentines Series

51. The highland boundary fault which extends from Stonehaven to Helensburgh, passes through Loch Lomond here at *Balmaha* on the east shore, and Arden on the west. The pass of Balmaha is a rugged and steep defile of about 250 metres in length, and during droving days was the gateway to the Highlands. Through this pass the McGregors would drive their stolen cattle, the narrow opening of which could be successfully defended by one or two adept swordsmen from those who would dare to follow them. At the foot of the pass is the old toll-house of 'Passfoot' shown above. The building has since been altered and extended, and at one time was a tea-room. One of the barges used for transporting the wood in connection with the liquor works can be seen below the toll-house. The jetty shown above no longer exists. Just beyond the headland on the far left, and opposite Inchcailloch, is the old pier, built 1905, and closed down in 1971 due to damage caused by the 546 ton paddle-steamer *The Maid of the Loch*. Two and a half miles north of here at Strathcashel point are the ruins of the Iron-Age fort of Cashel, offshore from which when the water level is low, can be seen the wooden beams of a crannog, which was built around the same time.

52. Balmaha was named after St. Mayhew or Maha, who reputedly had a healing well in the vicinity. In the middle of this view can be seen the stockpiles of wood, felled from the Montrose Estates on Lomondside and used in the production of acetid acid liquor. The works, which closed in 1920, were just out of shot on the far left, the buildings of which are nowadays the main village store. Tourism has superseded vinegar production as the mainstay of the local economy. Hidden among the buildings on the top right is an oak tree which is reckoned to be around a thousand years old. On the top left is the Duchess of Montrose Holiday Home opened on 2nd May 1891. This outdoor centre was to provide a holiday for the poor children of Glasgow, who would also be issued with clothing during their stay here. These days this building caters for Strathclyde Youth Club Association. Beyond the Montrose Home can be seen a smaller part of the ancient forest of Garaban. On the bottom left of this view is the 'Violet', one of the yachts belonging to the Dukes of Montrose. On its way to the breaker's yard between the wars, it foundered on a sandbank on the River Leven at Balloch, and its fittings and furniture became the prey of souvenir hunters.

Buchanan Schoolhouse and School - Milton of Buchanan

Shall send you more P.P.C.'s of surrounding district later on.

53. *St. Kentigerna* ('Kind Lady'), who was mother of St. Fillan and sister of St. Congan, was alleged to have had the ability to perform miracles. She founded a nunnery on *Inchcailloch* ('isle of the nuns or old women') where she died in 733 AD. Four centuries later a *Romanesque* church was built on the site of her grave. Parishioners would row (or swim) from the mainland to attend services at what became *Inchcailloch Parish Church*. By the 1620's the church was in a sorry state, but the Buchanan lairds, who had their own church, refused repeated demands for repair, with the result that by 1643 the church was abandoned and the parishioners attended the Buchanan's pre-reformation church of St. Mary's, during which period the parish changed its name to *Buchanan*. The present Buchanan Parish church was built in 1764 and it incorporated some of the masonry of the old Chapel of St. Mary. The tombstones were also brought over to the new site in this village of *Milton of Buchanan*, the burial place of the Dukes of Montrose, who, since 1932, reside locally at *Auchmar*. The church suffered a fire in 1938 whereby an ancient 8-sided font used at Inchcailloch was lost.

Buchanan Castle

Valentines Series

54. Supposed to be descended from a son of the king of Ulster, who landed in Argyll about 1016, Anselan was rewarded by Malcolm II for his services against the Danes by granting him the lands of Buchanan. His descendants later took the surname of Buchanan, their chief seat being on Clairinsh Island. The Buchanans were later granted the privilege of holding courts of life and limb on their estate by the Earls of Lennox, provided that any executions be carried out on the gallows of Catter, near Drymen, which was one of the chief seats of the Earls of Lennox. After 600 years on Loch Lomondside, the Buchanans lost their lands due to the death of the 22nd laird in 1682 without an heir or a will. The lands were then acquired by the 3rd Marquis, later Duke, of Montrose, a member of the Graham family who moved here from Mugdock Castle. A later Duke employed the famous gardener 'Capability' Brown to landscape the estate with rich woodlands. The old Buchanan House of 1724 was burned down during Christmas 1852, and by 1854 the above mansion, designed by William Burn, was built. Rudof Hess was a 'quest' here in 1941.

Market Square, Drymen

55. The name Drymen is a corruption of *Drummen*, meaning a 'ridge or knoll'. It gave its name to the Drummond family, ancestors of the Dukes of Perth, who lived in the area between the 12th and 14th centuries. There were two main reasons for Drymen's growth: the first was the acquisition of the Buchanan country (i.e., most of the eastern shore of Loch Lomond) by the Dukes of Montrose after 1682, who then settled down to live on the outskirts of the village in Buchanan Castle, and the second reason was the fact that the village lay on the Military Road between Dumbarton and Stirling, which was constructed in the 1750's. The buildings shown in the above view were built a number of years after the construction of the Military Road, and they encompassed the Market Square. This 1899 view shows the square being used as a cattle market. Alas, it has been many years since Drymen Square has seen livestock of any description. The square has been landscaped and trees now flourish where once many a farmer clinched deals. The pile of boulders on the left was the site of an old well. Modernisation has taken place within the square, the southern side of which has been rebuilt.

213001 J.V.   MAINS CASTLE AND KILMARONOCK HOUSE, DRYMEN.

56. Depending on etymology, *Kilmaronock* may mean either the church of St. Marnock *or* of St. Ronan. In January 1324, Robert the Bruce granted Kilmaronock Church to Cambuskenneth Abbey 'in propria usus'. In 1329, the year of Bruce's death, Malcolm, 5th Earl Lennox, granted Kilmaronock estate to Sir Malcolm Fleming, an ancestor of the Earls of Wigton, in recognition of his faithful service as custodian of Dumbarton Castle, a former Lennox stronghold. The estate passed via an heiress to Sir John Dennistoun in the mid-14th century. Through his friendship with Malcolm, 5th Earl Lennox, Bruce had taken an especial interest in The Lennox and its land-owners, an interest that was instilled into his son, David II, who granted infefment of the barony to Sir John Dennistoun for the annual payment of 4d. His family, in all probability, built the tower on the left of this 1931 view by Valentine. In 1404, Sir William Cunningham of Kilmaurs (an ancestor of the Earls of Glencairn), succeeded to the estates through marriage of an heiress. Later, William, 1st Earl Dundonald was in possession of the estates and whose family feued out the land.

57. The estate of *Ross Priory* was at one time part of the Kilmaronock estates of the Cunninghams from whom it was acquired by Walter Buchanan of Drumakill in 1624. As a result of activities during the 1715 rebellion, William Murray, Marquis of Tullibardine, lost the Dukedom of Athol to his younger brother. He became an outlaw after Culloden and sought protection of his friend, Buchanan of Ross, who secreted him in one of the vaulted underground chambers of Ross mansion. Fearing reprisals for harbouring a fugitive, Buchanan notified the authorities at Dumbarton. Betrayed, Tullibardine cursed Buchanan: 'There'll be Murrays at the Braes of Atholl when there's never a Buchanan at Ross,' a curse which appears to have been fulfilled by the end of the 18th century when heiresses fought for possession. The winner married her advocate, Hector MacDonald, who adopted the surname of Buchanan. During 1810-1815 he rebuilt Ross in the *Romantic* style of the period. Sir Walter Scott was a friend of this Hector MacDonald-Buchanan and became a regular visitor here in 1817 where he learned about Rob Roy's exploits and wrote part of *The Lady of the Lake*. This print shows Ross in 1829.

KILMARONOCK, LOCH LOMOND SIDE. (*South Shore*) W. T. MOLLISON, PHOTO PUBLISHER, ALEXANDRIA.

58. Two ancient churches existed in the parish of Kilmaronock: the 6th century St. Kessog's Church, the site of which may be marked by an ancient yew tree (NS 426875) on the road to Claddoch, and the other one kilometer north of Gartocharn, a pre-reformation church, near the ancient village of *Aber* (NS 430878; plundered by the vikings in 1263), which since the late 18th century has ceased to exist. From the adjacent harbour of *Townfoot* (NS 426877) and also from the quarries of *Ballagan*, east of Balloch, flagstones made of red sandstone were exported in 'scows' via the Leven and the Clyde to provide the 'plain-stanes' of the Trongate of Tobacco-Lord era Glasgow. On the left of this view is Duncryne or Duncruin (the hill of the witches), originally the property of Paisley Abbey: Inchmurren is named after Paisley's patron saint – St. Mirren. The hill was said to be the haunt of the Devil, the Lennox Fairies and the Lennox Witches. At the back of the hill, the Reformed Presbyterians met at a small church, a stone from which was built into the porch of Drymen U.P. Church. Gartocharn Primary School now occupy the foreground.

Loch Lomond (Frozen 1895.)

59. It is quite surprising to realise that such a large body of water as Loch Lomond is capable of being frozen. The first recorded freezing of the loch was in 1812 in one of the worst winters ever recorded in Europe. This was the year of Napoleon's Russian Campaign where he lost 400,000 of his half million invading army in the Russian winter. The most memorable freezing of the loch occurred in the winter of 1894-95: the frost set in on 28 December and by the beginning of February the loch was frozen its entire breadth for 10 miles; 30,000 skaters turned up; cyclists crossed to the islands. The Scottish Skating Championships were held at Duck Bay; a cricket match on skates took place opposite Cameron House, and shinty was played near Inchmurrin. The frozen-in steamers served as restaurants and coffee-stalls were set up, moving every now and again to prevent the braziers melting the ice. On the 3rd Saturday in February the sun came out and was so strong that skaters were overcome by the heat, and people even sunbathed on the ice! In the winter of 1961-62, wallabies imported by a local laird and encamped on an island, escaped over the ice south of Luss. Curiously, an Australian tourist knocked one down.

60. The first steamer to ply the loch was David Napier's *P.S. Marion* of 1817, a flat-bottomed wooden boat 60 ft by 13 ft wide with a 20 H.P. engine (similar to that of the *Comet*) with its huge funnel, almost as tall as the boat was long, which served as the mast. Daily at 6 a.m. the *P.S. Postboy* would leave Glasgow for Dumbarton to connect (via coach up the Vale of Leven) with the *Marion's* 10 a.m. sailing. The return trip would arrive in Glasgow at 8 p.m. The unreliable *Lady of the Lake* was set up in competition in 1825 but was beset with fatal drownings. The *Marion* was superceded by the *Euphrosyne* in 1828 (three years after the founding of the original Loch Lomond Steamboat Co.), being in turn superceded by the loch's first iron steamer, the *Loch Lomond* of 1838, which had the *Queen of Scots* as competition. In the 1840's, the *Waterwitch*, built locally at Pollochro, was a general purpose vessel carrying wood to the Paisley Mills via the Leven and the Cart to be made into bobbins; coal was brought on the return trip. Prior to 1850 when most of the piers were built, the old steamers would halt at places that were thought to appeal to tourists such as Rob Roy's Cave or Pulpit Rock.

Loch Lomond   S. S. "Princess May" at Balloch Pier

The Wrench Series No. 8102

61. That same year (1850) saw two steamers in competition: *Prince Albert* run by the New Loch Lomond Steamboat Co. and the short-lived *Pilot* run by the Caledonian & Dunbartonshire Railway Co. to compliment their then new rail link with Balloch. *Queen Victoria* replaced the *Waterwitch* in 1852 being itself superceded by the *Princess of Wales* in 1865, a companion to the 1857 *Prince of Wales* which had Queen Victoria as a passenger in 1859; ten years later Her Majesty was to sail on the *Prince Consort*, an 1862 replacement for the *Prince Albert* which had Empress Eugénie as a passenger in 1860. The *Queen (1886)* and the *Empress (1888)* were among the last of the Victorian steamers, being replaced in the Edwardian era by the quartet of two Princesses: the *Patricia* and *May* (the longest serving steamer at 55 years) and the two Princes: the *George* and *Edward*, the latter was to serve for 44 years till 1955. At first glance the members of this quartet appeared identical, there being only detail differences such as the numbers of portholes, or the design of the paddle-wheel housings. This quartet of steamers are the ones mainly featured on old picture postcards, their predecessors are only rarely featured.

62. The firm of William Stirling & Sons, textile printers, was established in 1750 at Dawsholm, Maryhill in Glasgow. Because of the purer water of the River Leven, the firm moved to the Renton, setting up the Cordale printfield works above Dalquhurn (1762), and the United Turkey Red Co. (1770), prosperous ventures which helped to establish the town of Renton. In 1791 £1,000 and a number of books were bequeathed by a member of the Stirling family to set up Stirling's Library in Glasgow. Another member of this family, James, bought Tullichewan Estate from the Colquhouns of Luss in 1792, erecting the castle shown in this view to a 'Gothic Picturesque' design by Lugar, who was later to design Balloch Castle (cf no.11). Subsequent owners of Tullichewan were the Horrocks family until 1843 when it was acquired by William MacOran Campbell, who, with his brother, Sir James, a former Glasgow Lord Provost, had founded the firm of J. and W. Campbell & Co. A son of Sir James, Sir Henry Campbell-Bannerman, served as Prime Minister during 1902-05. In 1922 the company amalgamated with another long-established company, Stewart & McDonald (1833) of Buchanan Street, forming *Campbell, Stewart & McDonald.*

Series 555-6.   **Argyll Motor Works, Alexandria.**   Davidson Brothers.

63. In 1896, Alexander Govan used the premises of a bicycle shop in Hozier Street, Bridgeton, Glasgow, to sell cars, which he later learned to assemble himself. He went one step better and built a car of his own – a prototype for his *Argyll Voiturette*, which he launched in 1900, selling 100 of them in his first year. Examples of these cars can be seen in *Glasgow Museum of Transport*. By 1905 he moved into these palatial premises. In 1907 Argyll Motors Ltd. held the record for European production and was granted a Royal Warrant from the King of Spain. That same year Govan died of food poisoning. (Nearby Govan Drive was named after him). Having lost Govan's driving force, the fortunes of the factory declined. In 1912/13 they were involved in a costly lawsuit over patent infringement with Daimler-Knight. The Argyll Co. won, but the lawsuit contributed to the company's liquidation in July 1914, though the old Hozier Street premises were still kept, where in 1920 a partially successful attempt to revive the production was made. In 1928 it was decided to call it quits. In 1935, the building became known as the *Torpedo Factory* under Admiralty control. The car in the forecourt of the Alexandria Works appears to be the 1911 'Flying-Fifteen'.

KILMAHEW CASTLE CARDROSS

64. The lands of *Kilmahew* – the church of Mahew or Macceus, a follower of St. Patrick – were granted to John Napier at the end of the 13th century by Malcolm, 5th Earl Lennox. Within the estate is *Kirkton of Kilmahew*, where a church dedicated to Mahew was known to exist some time before 1370. Kilmahew church was rebuilt by Duncan Napier in 1467 and for two centuries it served as the local school. Restoration and reconsecration took place in 1955 after being in ruins for many years (NS 342786). The now ruined 15th century Tower House (one mile north-east of Cardross village) was built by George Napier, one of the 18 generations of Napiers who enjoyed lairdship of the estate, various portions of which were frittered away until 1820 when the Napiers lost possession. A relation of the Napiers, Colin Dunlop of Carmyle (whose descendants built a mansion, 1848, which later became a children's museum in what is now Tollcross Park, Glasgow) was one of the originators of Glasgow's *Ship Bank*. James Burns of Bloomhill, who with his youngest brother George had set up a steam navigation business in 1824, acquired Kilmahew by about 1858. James Burns' son, John Wm., (who built the mansion shown here to a design by John Burnet) was one of the founders of the *Cunard Line*.

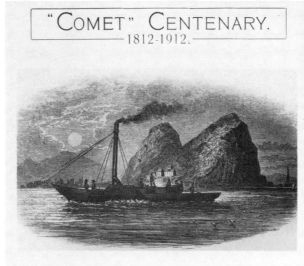

"COMET" CENTENARY.
— 1812-1912. —

THE "COMET," 1812.
The first steam vessel to carry passengers in Europe.

ENGINE OF THE "COMET."

0342

THE CLYDE OWES REMEMBRANCE TO THE PIONEERS.

HENRY BELL, THE INVENTOR.
JOHN ROBERTSON, THE MAKER OF THE ENGINE.

JOHN WOOD, THE BUILDER.
DAVID NAPIER, THE MAKER OF THE BOILER.

65. Both James Watt and the British Admiralty pooh-poohed Henry Bell's idea of steam navigation despite Lord Nelson's backing. Later, witnessing Symington's *Charlotte Dundas* on the Forth & Clyde canal, Bell was convinced that he should continue to persevere and he set-to with plans for a 42′ steam vessel capable of 7½ mph to be called the *Comet*. After viewing the plans, American-Scot Robert Fulton cribbed a few ideas resulting in the launch of the *Clermont* on the Hudson in 1807. Comet's 3hp engine was made by John Robertson at Dempster Street off north Frederick Street, Glasgow; the funnel by Pettigrew's smithy at the north-west corner of Sauchiehall and Buchanan Streets, Glasgow; the boiler and castings by David Napier, Dumbarton; built and launched at the Port Glasgow yard of John Wood. The maiden voyage from Broomielaw to Greenock in August 1812 was witnessed by many who expected it to blow up! Within a few years the Comet was outclassed by competition despite the addition of an 8hp motor shown here, and being lengthened 20′.

QUEEN'S HOTEL, HELENSBURGH.

66. Bell's talents were much in demand since setting up a successful Glasgow building business in 1790: he had become Helensburgh's first Lord Provost, 1807-09; he built a flourmill in Partick, Glasgow; Melville Ct. near Glasgow Cross; and rebuilt Dalmonach Print Works, Alexandria, after the 1812 fire. He was also a visionary: he proposed land reclamation around Loch Lomondside; a canal between east and west Tartert, Loch Fyne; a reservoir for Helensburgh centred round Kilbride in Glen Fruin (see 18); and a canal at Suez over sixty years before Ferdinand de Lesseps, who designed the present canal in 1869. In 1808 a Joint Stock Co. was set up to build the *Baths*, later *Queen's*, *Hotel*, with Bell as the building supervisor. The Stock Co. abandoned the hotel after it was built, selling it to Bell, who resold it to Archibald Smith of Jordanhill, with Bell and his wife as tennant proprietors. Bell's brother, Tom, operated the Baths Hotel-Dumbarton-Glasgow coach, stopping at Bowling Inn for 'spiritual' comfort on the way. The baths were at the basement, which later became the wine cellar. Since 1984 this building became the centrepiece of a luxury development called *Queen's Court* (East Clyde Street).

Ardencaple Castle   Helensburgh

67. The McAuleys of Ardencaple were descended from one of the sons of Alwyn, 2nd Earl of Lennox (13th century). When their first castle was built it was on a promontory with the sea on two sides. The castle was rebuilt in the 16th century during Walter McAuley's chiefship. Under his successor, Sir Auley, the family was at the peak of their prosperity, being feudal landlords with properties extending from Garelochhead to Cardross. After the Glenfruin massacre, the McAuleys turned their backs on the McGregors in order to escape conviction. For the next century and a half, the family fortunes declined, and various portions of the estates were sold off. The last Laird of McAuley sold the castle to the 4th Duke of Argyll when the roof fell in; he took refuge at Faslane. Inevitably, Faslane too was sold off to the Campbells and the now landless laird took shelter at High Laggernie above Rhu where he died in dejection (1767). Ardencaple was extended by Lord Frederick Campbell. After a fire in 1830, the 7th Duke of Argyll rebuilt the castle as shown. Sir James Colquhoun took possession in 1862. It became McAuley property again, albeit briefly, in the 1920's when Mrs. McAuly Stromberg acquired it. After its use by the Admiralty, it was demolised in 1957-59.

ROW PIER AND GARELOCH *This is the pier to which you come & the ships boats have the steam at the end.*

68. The village of Rhu was the centre of illicit smuggling, mostly whisky, in the 18th and early 19th centuries, the contraband being hidden in *Whistler's Glen*, so named because a whistle was given when the excisemen were in the vicinity. In Victorian times the older folk would talk with total sincerity about the merry fairies who were seen dancing in the glen! On a more serious note, around the 1820's the village was taken aback by the *Rhu Heresy* whereby Reverend John McLeod Campbell was deposed for preaching 'doctrines contrary to scripture and the confession of faith'. Campbell's deposition has since been considered a travesty of justice. Another controversial character was Madeleine Smith who had a country home at Rowaleyn (later renamed Invergare). She was charged with murdering her suitor, Langelier, with arsenic-laced cocoa. A 'not proven' verdict was returned. Above the two figures on the left can be seen the old training ship *Empress*. In recognition of Henry Bell's contribution to steam navigation, Robert Napier erected a stone effigy adjacent to Bell's grave in the churchyard. The stone pier shown here dates back to 1835, part of which still exists among the land reclaimed from the sea, the site now part of a marina where the *Opposition*, Ted Heath's renamed *Morning Cloud*, used to be berthed.

Shandon Hydropathic, Gareloch.

1880's

RELIABLE [W&S] SERIES.

69. Robert Napier was a cousin to David Napier who had built up an engineering works at Parkhead in Glasgow's east end. It was David Napier who built the *P.S. Marion* (1817) the first steamer to ply Loch Lomond. In 1822 Robert took over the concern. In 1833, he acquired land at Shandon, where he had a mansion built to a design by J. T. Rochead; it took twenty years to build and became one of the largest mansions in Scotland, incorporating a museum and art gallery featuring works by Rembrandt and Raphael. In the 1850's Napier was acknowledged as one of the world's most influential engineers, having built up such concerns as the Vulcan foundry, Lancefield Works, and Govan Shipyard. One of Napier's employees at Parkhead was William Beardmore who eventually rose to take control of the forge, which became one of the largest works in Scotland, employing 40,000 people. (A £20 million shopping centre is under construction on the site of the Camlachie/Parkhead Forge.) After Napier's death in 1879, West Shandon became a hydropathic and health resort. Designated a military hospital during the Second World War, it was soon taken over by the army. The adjacent military port at Faslane helped to seal its fate and it was demolished a century after it was built.

Shandon, Gareloch, From Pier.

70. After the conversion of Napier's mansion at Shandon into a hydro in the 1880's, the area became an attractive proposition for the well-to-do of Glasgow society. A 'ribbon development' of mansions and villas thus sprang up along 3 miles of coastline. At one time the inhabitants had the cheapest gas-lighting in Scotland (supplied from Helensburgh). To serve the area, a pier was built at Balernock in 1878, soon superceded by the more central Shandon pier, shown here, in 1886, replacing a previous adjacent structure of about 1860. The pier was closed down in 1967. The Gareloch, only 7 miles in length, once boasted eight piers. The Clyde Coast at the height of the era of going *doon the watter* had well over 100 piers of which barely ten remain in use today. The *Old Shandon Church* was built soon after the *Disruption* of 1843, whereby the Free Church split from the Established Church. Being derelict for years, plans are underway for its conversion into four flats. Like the pier, the spire, minaret, and the villa to the left of the church have gone, and the road re-aligned. The War Memorial, which used to be in front of the door, is in storage awaiting a new site. Behind the two figures is the Kirk Brae, with the old schoolhouse immediately behind the spire.

Faslane Chapel, Garelochhead.

71. One of the strongholds of the *Earls of Lennox*, the 12th century *Faslane Castle*, used to be situated about ¼ mile north of this chapel. The castle was impregnable, being at the junction of two deep glens (NS 249901). To this castle *William Wallace* came after destroying Rosneath Castle, and was warmly welcomed by the patriot Malcolm, 5th Earl of Lennox. By 1543, the castle was bestowed upon Adam Colquhoun who feued out portions of the estate; by 1693 the castle was attached to the Ardincaple Estates of the McAulays, who were descendants of the early Lennox Earls. The last laird of McAulay retreated to Faslane when the roof of Ardincaple Castle fell in. No trace of Faslane Castle has existed since the railway was laid through to Garelochhead. *Faslane Chapel*, dedicated to St. Michael, was probably built in the 14th century by the Earls of Lennox for their own use. The future husband of Mary Queen of Scots, *Lord Darnley*, whose family inherited the Lennox estates after the partition of the earldom, was said to have been baptised in the chapel, which has been in ruins since the Reformation. Stones from the chapel were used for building purposes by nearby Faslane Farm.

Garelochhead Hotel and Pier.

72. On Blaeu's map of 1654, *Garelochhead* is shown as *Loch gerr* – head of the short loch – a name not intended to contrast with nearby Loch Long, from Loch *Loung* or *Longue* – the ship loch. A stone jetty had been a fixture at Garelochhead for generations until replacement by a pier in 1845 built by McFarlane of Faslane; it became the scene for the *Battle of Garelochhead Pier* one Sunday in August 1853. The local laird, James Colquhoun, disapproved strongly of Sunday sailings. With his retinue, he barricaded the pier to prevent the *P.S. Emperor* from berthing, but he had not reckoned on the grim determination of the crew who let fly with anything that came to hand, such as vegetables, bottles, crockery, coal, etc., forcing the laird's contingent to retreat. A much larger pier, featured in this view, was built in 1879, rendering redundant the adjacent old pier which was dismantled in 1881. Only a portion of the 1879 pier now remains and is in a dangerous state of repair. Monday 29th January 1917 was a date that would be deeply etched in local memory: during acceptance trials, the *K13* submarine sank with loss of 34 lives, including 6 from the builders, Fairfields. The bravery of Commanders *Goodhart* who died, and *Herbert* saved the 47 others.

A CLACHAN AT LOCH LONG.

73. Loch Lomond may have 'the Bonnie Banks', but the 'Bonnie Shore' belongs to North Portincaple. The building in this view is the romantic-looking yet utilitarian *Tigh-na-Clachan* with fishing nets drying on the shore. A different type of 'fishermen' lived north of here – whalers at Glenmallan. In the days before the building of the *Rest and be Thankful road* through Glencroe by General Wade in 1768, Portincaple was of strategic importance in travelling to and from Argyll, accomplished by ferry via Lochgoilhead. Drovers coming from Argyll would bring their cattle via *Argyle's Bowling Green* to *Mark cottage*, the loneliest cottage in the Highlands, where the cattle were forced to swim across to Portincaple. At Whistlefield, above Portincaple, is the inn frequented by drovers; and at Portincaple are the ruins of the building used to stable the traveller's horses overnight. It was to the hillside above Whistlefield and Garelochhead that the Colquhouns intended to meet the McGregors, before being ambushed on the boggy ground of Glen Fruin in 1603. Students had gathered on the isthmus to watch the battle, but were herded for their own safety into a shack on Greenfield moor. There they were stabbed to death.

Loch Long, "Susie's Castle", Portincaple.

74. A man's (or for that matter a woman's) home is his (her) castle. Jimmy and Susie Reid, who were 'travelling folk', ingeniously used an old upturned boat covered in oilskin and canvas to solve their housing problem. It was more spacious (and more permanent) than the tents which one would associate with travelling folk. Being very houseproud, clay-pipe smoking Susie always kept her 'castle' very tidy and immaculate. The boat on the left is testimony of Jimmy's occupation: he was a fisherman who sold his catch locally. To supplement her income after her husband's death, Susie grew her own vegetables and worked as a domestic; she would also have postcards of herself published to sell to curious tourists (and charged tourists who took her photograph). These postcards, of which the above is an example, now adorn post-card collections world-wide. It became a tradition with her to sell oranges at Garelochhead on New Year's Day. In later years Susie had her home surrounded by a wall and a wire fence to give the effect of having a garden. She was in her 70's when she died. After her death, *Susie's Castle* was burned down to prevent occupation by vagrants. (NS 232937.)

Rosneath House.

990/20

75. The barony of Rosneath (Rhos noeth – the bare or unwooded promontory) belonged in the 12th century to one of the sons of Alwyn, the 2nd Earl Lennox. Through Alwyn's marriage to Lady Eva, a daughter of Gilchrist, Earl Menteith, the estate passed into Menteith ownership sometime during the reign of David I (1124-53). The castle built by Alwyn's son in the early 12th century was destroyed by William Wallace towards the end of the 13th century. When the Campbells of Argyll took possession of the estate in the 15th century, they substantially rebuilt the castle, and later enlarged it in 1630. Thomas Mylne was commissioned to add castellations and other improvements in 1784 by the 5th Duke Argyll. This ancient pile burned down in 1802, so the 5th Duke employed the services of Joseph Bonomi the Elder to build the castle shown in this view (1803-06), described by Neale as 'the most chaste and correct specimen of its style in the kingdom'. Princess Louise, a daughter of Queen Victoria, came into possession of the estate through her marriage to the Marquis of Lorne, heir to the Dukedom of Argyll, in 1871. As Princess Louise died without issue, the estate was sold after her death in December 1939. The castle was blown up in 1961 (NS 270822).

Rosneath, Adam & Eve.

76. These are the celebrated Silver Fir trees which were located near the site of the old mansion of the Campbells of Carrick at Camsail on the Rosneath Peninsula. Conjecture has it that they were among the first Silver Firs ever planted in Britain, presumably that is the reason for the epithet of 'Adam and Eve'. It is on record that a Silver Fir was planted in 1603 in Harefield Park, Middlesex, and these trees may date from around the same time. A drawing in Strutt's *Sylva Britannica* (1829) showed one of these trees to be then around 90' high with a girth of 7'7". Lord Frederick Campbell stated that the trees were around 200 years old in 1835. By mid-Victorian times the trees were claimed to be the largest Silver Firs in Europe and as such were famous tourist attractions. Towards the end of the 19th century the trees were said to be past their best, and were dead by 1959. Also at Rosneath was an avenue of yew trees of immense age planted by the monks of a pre-reformation monastery. In the past there was another remarkable tree in the Lennox, but this time an ash tree at Bonhill. Near the beginning of the 18th century the interior of a large ash tree was gouged out, forming a small room 9'11" in diameter with a conical roof. It sat 18 people in a hexagonal bench, with a table in the middle. Entry was gained via a lockable door. The tree was in use for decades, and surprisingly, continued to thrive.